the Forty Martyrs

In crate uiminea positi, lorisque ligati, 5
Per ſaxa, ad furcas, et per loca fœda trahuntur.
Carnifices laqueos, cultrósque, ignésque, parant

Tied to hurdle, captive is dragged to execution.

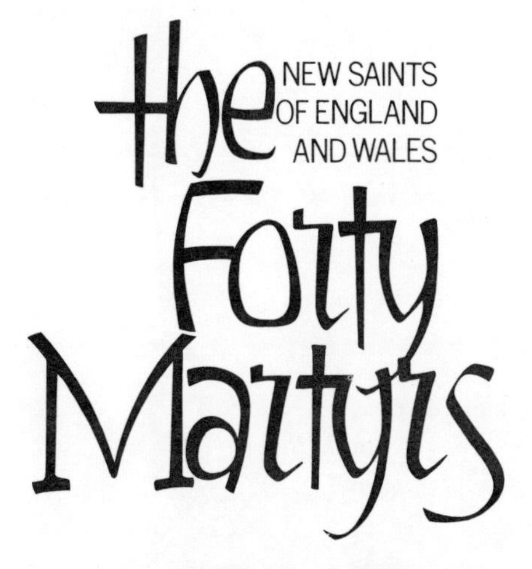

by DONALD W. WUERL

With a Preface by Cardinal John Wright

OUR SUNDAY VISITOR INC.

Huntington, Indiana 46750

NIHIL OBSTAT:

Rev. Lawrence Gollner
Censor Librorum

IMPRIMATUR:

+Leo A. Pursley, D.D.
Bishop of Fort Wayne-South Bend

Library of Congress Catalog Card Number: 70-160365

Illustrations from the article, Martyrs of England and Wales in the New Catholic Encyclopedia. Used with permission of the Catholic University of America, Washington, D.C.

Published, printed and bound in the U. S. A. by
OUR SUNDAY VISITOR INC.
Noll Plaza, Huntington, Indiana 46750

807

Contents

Ad breue ſuſpenſi tempus, cum morte ſecunda
Confligunt: ferròque armatus uiſcera tortor
Eruit, et flammis mandat: ſed membra, caputque
Diſſecat, et contis ſumma ad pinnaculâ figit

Cut down and quartered; heart thrown into fire.

Preface

FATHER Donald Wuerl has done readers in the English speaking world a great service by bringing together biographical notes concerning the forty English Martyrs. For one dreadful moment, it seemed that no one knew who they were or anything about them except that they died, in some obscure manner, about 400 years ago and came from England and Wales. Very few people knew the names of more than a few of them and, there seemed to be something close to a reluctance to acknowledge not only how but why they were put to death. It was this strange state of affairs that made me, among many, welcome Father Wuerl's venture into research on their biographies and prompted me to write, with no apologies for its polemical spirit, the brief essay which now serves as a Preface to these biographical notes.

Every devout Catholic, I dare say everyone who claims the name of Christian or who senses the dignity of what it is to be a conscientious person of whatever integral commitment, rejoiced in the news from Rome of the canonization of the forty English and Welsh martyrs.

There are inevitable shadings in the reasons for rejoicing with respect to canonizations. Such is the case when a mere girl is canonized, like Maria Goretti. Such is the case in the canonization of saints from the Third World, from nations or tribes which, in our limited vision, we sometimes see as beyond the frontiers of what, for cultural rather than theological reasons, we have tended to think of as the Christian world. Such is the case when a great social worker is canonized, or a saint who happens to be a surpassing scholar (or *vice versa*), or a witness to a special virtue seemingly more relevant and more "popular" in centuries gone by and lands afar.

So, too, in the case of the forty English and Welsh martyrs. The reasons for rejoicing in their canonization are nuanced and not without differences. There are not a few who rejoice that the Holy See, without compromising its ecumenical aspirations and proper spirit of openness to new hopes and directions among all Christians, has acted with what appears to them to be a certain boldness, not to say defiance of the mood of the hour, in proclaiming the special excellence of these men and women who dared to be different, refusing to conform with the demands of the hour and the expectations of what turned out to be the "majority."

There is, in fact, small reason for special rejoicing under this heading. If the Holy See were to be forgetful of those who bore such historic witness to that See and to all the premises on which it rests, she would be forgetful of the very promises of Christ by which she is sustained and her special mission to proclaim and to praise fidelity to those promises in order to raise up new future good servants of the King or the community, to be sure, but of Christ and His Kingdom first.

Others rejoice in the canonization because they see in it, very properly, a salute by the Universal Church to the lonely place of a right conscience in the midst of the tumult of disputations and the chaos of changing times, cultures and moral codes. Many—I confess to be among these—rejoice in the simultaneous canonization of a litany of martyrs which includes laymen and clergy, men and women, priests diocesan and religious, artistocrats and simple folk, in a word, a cross-section of representatives of all who constitute the strength and the variety of a land that speaks our English tongue.

Some, more narrowly, may take particular delight precisely in the fact that these saints are English, "some of our own, at last!" I was in St. Peter's when Thomas More and John Fisher were canonized these many years ago and I shall never forget the mingled sentiments of amusement and yet holy joy with which I heard a good woman from Liverpool, all of us lost in the mob far nearer the obelisk of St. Peter's Square than the altar of St. Peter's Basilica, reply to her husband when he announced from his perilous vantage point on the base of a column that the Pope had just read the bull declaring the canonization of More and Fisher: "Thank God there are now saints in heaven who understand English!" I seconded the motion, but reflected that it was what they *said* in English, rather than their facility in the tongue, that won for them the honors of the altar.

Our Holy Father, Pope Paul, has given his own reasons for rejoicing in an address to the College of Cardinals May 18, 1970. He speaks of his "great joy" and "own wish" as he reports the unanimous petition of the Consistory to salute as saints the martyrs of England and Wales whose canonization he then fixed for October 25. He then sets forth the special reasons for his joy and his wish, as well as for the "highly appropriate" timing of the canonization. He sees in their recognition "a most effective way of promoting the good of the Church, at a time when she is making every endeavor to bring back unity to all Christians, and to maintain and strengthen those common human and Christian values whose existence is being threatened by the encroachments of materialism."

He reveals that he is not unmindful of the argument that these martyrs died in times of a confusion and a spirit perhaps different to those in our own day and he repudiates any intention of opening up old wounds or adding to the bewilderment of our times by recalling controversies now dormant, at least, and even, please God, dead. Nonetheless, putting fully aside the rancors of the past and its memories of sorrow, the Holy Father insists that the present canonizations are filled with lessons for the future:

"First of all, they are a shining example of that genuine faith, which will have nothing to do with ambiguity or false compromise in whatever is held as sacred: a faith is a necessary condition of all true and fruitful ecumenical dialogue.

"At the same time, these martyrs are especially noteworthy as examples of true Christian charity towards those who do not profess the same Christian faith. In an age when religious controversy stirred up so much hatred, it is most heart-warming to notice that such attitudes are completely foreign to these heroes of the Christian faith. Rather the reverse, as the acts of their marytrdom witness: many of them showed themselves as only too ready to surrender their lives with the greatest willingness for the spiritual welfare of their fellow countrymen.

"Finally, we cannot pass over in silence the fact that this canonization is most opportune for another reason, and it is this: Today, materialistic and naturalistic philosophies of life are gaining ground and are threatening to deprive us of the spiritual heritage of our civilization. These blessed martyrs, who did not hesitate to sacrifice their very lives in obedience to the clear voice of conscience and the will of God, are a glowing testimony to human dignity and liberty. And their witness is all the more precious since it comes from a group of men and women representing so many different walks of life."

Considerations, perhaps, of personal delicacy and official reserve may have suggested to the Holy Father that he abstain from explicit exposition of the substance, content and precise point of the "precious witness" to which these so many and different English and Welsh martyrs gave their love, their example and their lives. That witness was to the claims of the Holy Father himself, the special primacy of Peter and his successors, the unique place in the Universal Church of the Apostolic See of Rome. Unless this be clear in all considerations of the case, the story is without point and the witness unto martyrdom is in vain. The forty martyrs whose memory rejoices us in these occasionally melancholy times are witnesses to the *Romanità*, properly understood and never to be downgraded, of authentic Catholicism in England. That *Romanità* dates from England's own Augustine. It is proclamied in the patronage of so many of her Cathedrals, monasteries, religious institutions. Its presence, often forgotten but never destroyed, abides in some of England's proudest traditions and happiest phrases: Defender of the Faith is only one.

There are, therefore, those of us who particularly rejoice in the present canonizations because they reaffirm, dramatically and unforgettably, the ties with Rome and with the Bishop of Rome which have never ceased to characterize, with a fervor rarely found elsewhere, the Catholicism of England. Those ties are not political nor, except in certain humanistic elements, merely cultural. They do not reveal themselves only in exuberant proclamations *From the Flaminian Gate* or in prophetic hopes of a *Second Spring* of Catholicism in England, dismissed by the unthinking as romantic, poetic gestures. They are not inconsistent with any of the essential elements of the native English genius; quite the contrary. They are summed up in the word *Romanita,* not as it is mocked in contemporary cocktail discussions of theology, but as it was profoundly operative in the witness of the English martyrs and remains operative in English Catholicism's loyalty to the Roman Magisterium as well as its own traditions of Catholic faith.

I venture to add a further perhaps official but also, I feel, deeply personal reason for rejoicing in these canonizations. That reason derives from the nature of the post it is my privilege to hold as Prefect for the Congregation for the Clergy and from the fact that I am a priest. The priests in the list of the newly canonized martyrs are, like Thomas More, men for all seasons. They are, unmistakably, men for our own times. In the midst of the grimness and lack-luster standardization of our society in so many of its aspects, they strike a note of joy, urbanity, humanism, hope, unconquerable faith and conquering love. They represent the English priesthood at its best, which, for me, has meant, since first I came to know English priests over thirty years ago, the Catholic priesthood in its finest expression. In this alone I find ample reason for rejoicing in the recent Roman ceremonies.

One of the martyrs, Edmund Campion, anticipated the grounds of my rejoicing when he said: "There will never want in England men that will have care of their own salvation, nor such as shall advance other men's. Neither shall this Church here ever fail, so long as priests and pastors shall be found for their sheep, rage man or devil never so much."

Another, Ralph Sherwin of the Venerable English College in Rome, reflected the spirit which rejoices me when, with typical British understatement and wry humor, he described the clanking of the chains which throughout his captivity bound his feet: "I wear now on my feet and legs some little bells to keep me in mind who I am, and Whose I am. I never heard such sweet harmony before."

But no one proclaimed more proudly what the priests of the British Isles thought of themselves, their dignity, their special vocation and their relationship both to time and to eternity (I speak of the days before sacerdotal "identity crisis") than did the Welshman David Lewis. No mere doctrinnaire theologian or priest by social position and Catholic by family inheritance, he was known as *Tady Tlodion* (Father of the Poor). Let his words, uttered in the moment of his martyrdom, sum up the special reasons for priestly rejoicing which move my heart as I pen these lines:

"Here is a numerous assembly—may the great Savior of the world save every soul of you all. I believe you are here met not only to see a fellow-native die, but also to hear a dying fellow-native speak. My religion is the Roman Catholic; in it I have lived above these forty years; in it I now die, and so fixedly die, that if all the good things in this world were offered me to renounce it, all should not remove me one hair's breadth from my Roman Catholic faith. A Roman Catholic I am; a Roman Catholic priest I am; a Roman Catholic priest of that religious order called the Society of Jesus I am; and I bless God who first called me. I was condemned for reading Mass, hearing confessions, and administering the sacraments. As for reading the Mass, it was the old, and still is the accustomed and laudable liturgy of the holy Church; and all the other acts are acts of religion tending to the worship of God, and therefore dying for this I die for religion."

JOHN CARDINAL WRIGHT
Vatican City

En quos Presbyteros pretio corruptus Iudas
Prodidit, aut pœnis legum conterritus hospes:
Funibus implicitos, claudendos carcere, custos
Accipit, in limbos et tetra ergastula trudens.

Informer identifying priest and the march to prison.

Introduction

On Sunday, October 25, 1970 in the midst of the solemn ceremonies in St. Peter's Basilica and before a huge crowd of Roman, British and other faithful, Pope Paul VI read the decree that confirmed for the Church still struggling here on earth that 40 more of God's children and our brothers now live in the presence of God. There is no way to capture on paper the excitement and joy that filled St. Peter's on that bright, clear Fall morning. The whole church was alive. The great Renaissance monument of marble and bronze became unmistakably a temple of the Living God. In it resounded the voices of thousands of believers united in faith, charity and prayer. This was an atmosphere of joy and triumph that well reflected our faith that Christ is risen and we are called to join Him in a new life that has no end. Here did the Holy Father's proclamation seem both timely and encouraging. "Some of us have made it" might sum up the feelings of so many of the believers who cheered the Pope's declaration.

The Church through its living visible head had stated in formal and definitive manner what most of those acquainted with the lives of the English martyrs already took for granted, that the men and women who died professing their faith left this world as God's chosen ones—beloved by Him. The formal canonization merely opened to all the

Church the opportunity to re-affirm the virtue and glory of these selected faithful. We all live in the hope of someday being united perfectly with Christ. It is for this reason and on this hope that we can rejoice when the Church is now certain that one unique group of fellow believers has reached what St. Paul calls "our goal." The declaration that these Forty Martyrs live with the Master as we hope someday to do is the essence of the canonization ceremony. The grasp of this simple message is basic to the understanding of the joy that fills St. Peter's at any canonization.

But there were aspects of the October 25 celebration that indicated other parochial causes for such an outpouring of love and joy. Cardinal Heenan, Archbishop of Westminster, in an article for the "Catholic Fireside" noted why the English found this event so wonderful. For a minority that has fought for 400 years to keep its faith, the recognition of some of those who died in the battle can only be greeted with cheers and tears. He continues, "The Martyrs died to preserve the Mass in this country and to defend the authority of the Vicar of Christ." Is there any wonder that this portion of God's people should so rejoice standing in the presence of the same Vicar at the Mass which acclaims their countrymen holy.

For others the joy of the canonization was also that of a work well done. Father Paul Molinari, S.J., the postulator in Rome of the cause of the Forty, and Father Clement Tigor, the vice-postulator in England saw the decree as the final stone in a building on which they had worked with countless others for years. They had collected, sifted, compiled and argued the facts and merits of the lives and deaths of these 40 for nearly half a lifetime.

Out of the great interest in both Rome and England that this canonization kindled has come much research into the lives of the martyrs. I have taken a few historical points for this introduction from that bounty of material on those men and women who died loyal citizens of the crown but God's children first. It is by no means an exhaustive work as its size indicates nor is it more than a brief review of some of the incidents surrounding the deaths of those called to God's glory under the reign of several English monarchs over a 150-year period.

John Cardinal Wright has been most kind in providing a Preface to this book in which he gives another dimension to the facts in the narrative. With his own insight into the lives and times both of the 16th century England and the 20th century modern world, he has given fresh understanding to the often repeated facts. The Preface gives heart and life to the skeleton which history tends to be.

Captos dum celebrant, in ſacro lictor amictu
Raptat per medias populo insultante plateas.
Capti rure alij, manibus pedibúſque ligati
Imponuntur equis, primásque uehuntur adurbes

Priest captured saying Mass then led to the Tower.

The Approaching Storm

OSBERT Lancaster relates in his small work "Drayneflete Revealed" the discretion of one of the Fidget family, Sir Jonas Fidget, when it came to matters of the faith. He was noted as a "sincere friend of the reformed faith, except for a short period under Queen Mary when he momentarily lapsed into his old ways." Faced with the changes of the times and the uncertainty of the future of the old faith many a man followed this same path of discretion. Henry the king ruled and was in no mood to be disobeyed. Few found reason to dispute him, particularly if it meant death. And death was exactly the price being exacted from all who challenged the new religion. For those clever enough to read the sign of the times Henry had other rewards. In speaking of Post-Reformation Drayneflete, Lancaster writes: "The most important result of the reform of religion in Drayneflete was the disappearance of the Priory and the erection on its site (and with much of its material) of the magnificent Tudor mansion of the Fidget family."

The tale of the religious upheaval that was a violent part of English history for over one hundred years goes back perhaps long before Henry VIII's reign. As a lingering, chronic fever that breaks the surface first in a rash and then in running sores, did the religious ferment in England grow under Henry, through Elizabeth until the final blood-letting of the Commonwealth of the Puritans and the short-lived restorations.

Henry VIII, the second of the Tudor family kings, had displayed both intelligence and shrewdness in his early days as king. His throne was secure or at least as secure as the English throne had been in some hundred-odd years since Richard II had been murdered. For a brilliant, if not entirely his own, defense of the faith against Martin Luther he had received for himself from Pope Leo X the title Defender of the Faith. Politically the realm was steady. Wolsey as chancellor had affairs well in hand. Culturally, after the winter imposed by the long Wars of the Roses, the signs of spring were beginning to show. Both Stephen Howes and John Skelton had published acceptable verse. Prosperity was evident and trade, the mother of English wellbeing, was, if in its infancy, healthy. Along with all this came a growing nationalism that was to bring so much division to Europe. But all that was still in the future; for the present, it meant that Englishmen were now beginning to see their first loyalty in their nation and themselves as Englishmen. This was no small thing for a land, like most of Europe, which once considered itself first in provincial terms and secondly, if at all, in terms of Christendom.

On to this stage stepped Anne Boleyn. The well rehearsed story of her part in the dissolution of the marriage of Henry and his lawful wife Catharine is news to no one. And with it came the wreck of a religious unity that had been England's heritage for over one thousand years.

Quite simply the case presented by Henry was that his original dispensation to marry Catharine was invalid. Henry was the younger brother of Crown Prince Arthur, first son of Henry VII and heir to the throne of England. Unfortunately Arthur died in his youth before reaching the throne. Equally unfortunately for the subsequent history of England, Arthur had married Catharine. Although they were rightfully and legally married, Arthur never lived with nor consummated his marriage to Catharine. It remained the treaty alliance between Spain, then in its ascendency, and England. Henry, upon the premature death of Arthur, claimed both the throne of England and his brother's wife. The desirability of the alliance remained.

After appeal to Rome, Henry obtained a dispensation granting him permission to marry Catharine. Here the trouble begins. Catharine and Henry had no trouble consummating the marriage as well as the alliance, but could not produce a son. Gradually, as time passed and no heir was born, Henry began to have second thoughts about his marriage to Catharine. His conscience bothered him. Or at least so he said in his letter to Rome asking the presently reigning Pope to declare that his predecessor on the chair of Peter had not the power to permit his marriage to Catharine. The Holy See turned down the request that the Pope declare that his predecessor had overstepped his bounds in exercising his authority over the Church. Given the position of the Holy See, Henry appealed to the theologians of his day, particularly those at the University of Paris. His question was a simple one. Who is right in the case of interpreting the application of the Pope's authority, the Pope or King Henry? The case, or rather his cause, dragged on as faculty was pitted against faculty. Finally Henry acted. All the verdicts were not in his favor.

Defiance was something new to King Henry. He would hear no argument that countered his own. Anne would be both wife and Queen with or without the Pope's invalidation of his previous marriage. It is at this point that the story of the forty martyrs, in fact, begins. Clement VII refused to give in to the demands forwarded him from London that the Church declare invalid the royal marriage of Henry and Catharine. After involved appeals and interminable discussions involving most of the greater universities of Europe, Henry married Anne. At the same time he had the new Archbishop of Canterbury, Cranmer, dissolve his first marriage leaving him free to secure the succession of his throne for any children he might have by Anne. Things moved rapidly from this point on.

Parliament confirmed Henry's divorce. The Pope excommunicated Henry. Henry enacted the Act of Supremacy, appointing himself and his successors Protector and only Supreme Head of the Church and clergy of England. Thus in 1534 the fight which had started as a quarrel over the need for an heir broke out into a full fledged struggle on doctrinal matters. The ancient Catholic tradition had maintained that there is but one Church spread over all the world and found in all the different nations. This Church was universal, hence its name Catholic. Within there were to be neither Jews nor Greeks, French nor English, but all Catholic. Within this Church on matters of faith and morals there was one supreme voice, that of Peter in his successors. From the Pope's decision on the faith there was no appeal. Against this the Act of Supremacy proposed a new doctrine. In England the Church was no longer to be considered the Church in England but of England. The king and he alone was the supreme head and therefore spokesman for the faith. The Holy See pronounced this heresy. Soon other doctrines were to be involved in the fight, most particularly the nature and sacrificial value of the Mass.

Suppression of Religious

As the battle lines were drawn up it became apparent that few were prepared to resist the king in his pretentions as Head of the Church. The most well known of those who did place first his faith was Thomas More. In 1535, one time Lord Chancellor of England and friend of the King, Sir Thomas More, who was "the king's loyal servant but God's servant first," was beheaded. Reminiscent of Becket's protest of submission to the king in all things "saving his sacred office and the rights of holy Church," many others were soon to follow this path to the scaffold, swordsman's block or the dungeon's tortures.

It is at this date that we meet the first of the group now known as the Forty English Martyrs. Fathers John Houghton, Augustine Webster and Robert Lawrence were all Carthusian priors. Houghton served as prior of the monastery at London, Webster at Axholme, Lincolnshire, and Lawrence at Beauvole. The three gathered in London in 1534 to petition the king for an exemption from the Oath of Supremacy for their communities. As if Houghton knew what fate would be his when he arrived to petition the king, he prepared himself with what seems to be almost a joyful anticipation. A special triduum of prayer was held at the monastery, at the conclusion of which this prior celebrated the Mass of the Holy Spirit. Then, together with Lawrence and Webster, he marched off to see the king. They asked a respite from the application of the new law called the Act of Supremacy, which held it to be high treason to deny that the king was supreme head of the Church of England. Their petition was based on the supposition that one could be both loyal subject of the crown and faithful son of the Church in England.

The answer to this request was imprisonment and trial for high treason. Thomas Cromwell, at this point, vice-regent in matters relating to the Church of England, conducted the trial and ordered the verdict of guilty. On May 4, 1535, the three were dragged off through the yards of the Tower of London to be ceremoniously executed before a large turn-out of the royal court. To emphasize the point that this was a break with the Church and not just the execution of a few treacherous monks the three were executed wearing their religious habits, a procedure openly repudiated by all the Christian nations of Europe for over seven hundred years.

That same day another religious who was outspoken in defense of the old faith met his death. Father Richard Reynold of the Brigittine Order was noted as perhaps the most learned monk of his time. Both his learning and his piety were remarked at Cambridge where he was a professor until, he, as spokesman for his order, refused to take the Oath of Supremacy. Writing of Reynold, Cardinal Pole, who knew him well and was himself no stranger in the groves of the academy, says this priest was the only English monk he knew who was well versed in the three classical languages, Latin, Greek and Hebrew. His knowledge of the Church fathers was in evidence as he pleaded his case in court. First he called on all the majority of the living faithful in England to be his witness to the truth of old religion over the new interpretation; then, as dead witnesses, he summoned "all the great General Councils, all historians, the holy doctors of the Church for the last fifteen hundred years, especially, St. Ambrose, St. Jerome, St. Augustine and St. Gregory." The trial ended in a vote of "guilty."

On June 2, 1957, on the grounds of Syon House, where once stood Syon Abbey, the first Mass in four centuries was celebrated and prayers offered in honor of its one-time prior, Richard Reynold.

Following this row with the English monasteries, Henry suppressed, in 1536, all the smaller or lesser religious houses within his kingdom, generously disposing of their land and possessions to his followers. In 1538 the same tactic was this time applied to all the larger remaining religious houses, thus rendering their protests politically and economically sterile.

John Stone, an Augustinian monk from Canterbury, took exception to the high-handed way with which he felt his order had been handled, and protested. This was not his first public admonition addressed to the king. But, it seems, this time he protested once too often; first against the divorce, then against the Act of Supremacy, and now against the suppression of the monasteries. In December 1538, nearly four centuries from the martyrdom of Becket at the same spot, when the friars refused to sign the deed of surrender of their home and possessions, John was arrested and committed to prison at Westgate. In retaliation for his recalcitrant behavior it was decreed that he should be hanged, drawn and quartered. This sentence passed on him was reserved only for the most hideous crimes such as conspiracy to do bodily harm to the king. Nevertheless it was imposed on this man because he did protest too much. The execution of this sentence usually required that the victim be dragged by horse to his place of death, then hanged by the neck with chains just short of his death, then cut down while still conscious, or at least still alive, chopped into four quarters, effectively terminating his life. So died John Stone. The manner of execution soon became a favorite applied to Catholic priests and of the Forty Martyrs so died Edmund Arrowsmith, a Jesuit, and Ambrose Barlow, a Benedictine.

Barlow was the fourth of fourteen children of Sir Alexander and Dame Barlow of Manchester. He was born at Barlow Hall on the outskirts of Manchester in the same year that it became unlawful, under the specific title of high treason, for a priest to be found within the realm. The same all-inclusive law named it a felony for anyone to receive or aid a priest. The young Barlow at the age of twelve became a page to a protesting kinsman. But later in his teens he returned to the faith and went to Douai to become a monk. His profession into that order followed the permission of the Benedictines obtained from the Pope to establish at Douai a monastery dedicated to St. Gregory the Great, Apostle of England.

After his ordination the young priest went on the English mission. First travelling to his family home at Barlow Hall and then to Astley, Barlow set up headquarters outside Manchester. Never in good health, he often found himself in great difficulty keeping up the schedule he set for himself of constant travel with several Masses each day in various parts of the countryside around his native city. A contemporary describes Father Barlow's Mass at Christmas at Morley's Hall, "in a venerable vestment that came out on great days, at the clean altar on which stood great wax candles made by himself. The picture before the altar was the arraignment of Our Savior. Afterwards they sang carols around the great fire, and had something hot to drink. The pastor and his penitents seemed to me to represent good Catholics in the primitive Church."

After the arrest of Father Edmund Arrowsmith, who was to die in the manner described above, Father Ambrose continued to gain access to him in prison and give him the sacraments. Soon Barlow was arrested. At the trial he pleaded that he was a priest and therefore a believer of the "ancient religion." His fate was that of many priests to follow. He was drawn on a hurdle from Lancaster Castle to his place of execution where he was hanged, disembowelled and quartered. The mortuary notice sent round to his Benedictine brothers asked that instead of a Requiem Mass they should offer Masses of the Holy Trinity in thanksgiving.

But all this happened after the death of Henry. Following marriages to Anne Boleyn, who was beheaded in 1536; Jane Seymour, who died in 1537; Anne of Cleves, divorced in 1540; Catharine Howard, beheaded in 1542; and Catharine Parr; Henry himself died. Within his reign Henry had himself appointed by the Act of Supremacy in 1534, "Protector and only Supreme Head of the Church and Clergy of England." One year later came the Tyndale's translation of the Bible into English under the authority of the king. Then came the Statute of the Six Articles defining as heresy any of the following Catholic positions: transubstantiation, communion in one kind for laymen, celibacy for the priesthood, inviolability of vows of chastity, validity of private Masses and necessity of auricular confession. In 1540 Thomas Cromwell, chief architect of the Henry-Anne of Cleves marriage, fell under the king's displeasure and the headsman's ax. Henry's death came on January 18, 1547. The king, who had destroyed the unity of a nation and the faith of a people for an heir, met death knowing that Parliament had already declared one of his daughter's, Elizabeth, illegitimate, and that Edward, his only male issue, was not too long for this world.

St. Edmund Campion

Elizabeth Continues the Martyrdoms

IN 1588 Elizabeth, termed Queen of England by the grace of God and Defender of the Faith, was proclaimed and crowned queen. The short and turbulent reigns of Edward VI, Mary, and the ten days of Lady Jane Grey, were over. The new faith was to be once more firmly installed. The Act of Supremacy and the Act of Uniformity were again proclaimed, soon to be followed by the adoption of the Thirty-Nine Articles in 1563. The Thirty-Nine Articles established a Church of England, largely Protestant in dogma but with a hierarchical organization similar to the Catholic, and a liturgy translated into English from the prevailing Latin.

Soon it was decided that firm steps had to be taken for things were getting out of hand. There was now not only the threat of the Catholic adherence to the old religion but the phenomenon within the new church of dissenters and non-conformists. Elizabeth saw in her realm the factions known as Puritans, who wished in their own terms to "purify" the Church; the Presbyterians, who planned to substitute organization by presbyters in place of bishops; the Brownists, who gave birth to the latter-day Congregationalists; and the Unitarians, who denied the doctrine of the Trinity. It soon became apparent that only harsh steps would bring all to the new religion. Masses and the recitation of the Divine Office were to be stopped. So declared the queen!

The thoroughness of Elizabeth's suppression of public Mass is reflected in a letter from an Italian nobleman in England to friends abroad. Dated June 27, 1559, he writes: "We have no longer Masses anywhere except in the houses of the French and Spanish ambassadors. All the friars and monks of every sort have received their passport; some of them have gone away, and will be followed by the others, although the Carthusians do not choose to depart till they are compelled to do so by force, which will soon be used."

With the passage of time and the increase in effort to persuade the English to accept the new religion the blood began to flow a little more freely. His Lordship Edwin Sandys, convert to the new viewpoint and recently appointed Archbishop of York, wrote of the stubbornness with which the people and lower clergy of England held to the ancient faith. In a letter, dated October 28, 1577, to the Privy Council, he wrote of his difficulties in "convincing" his flock of their need to change:

"I have already laboured what I can since my coming hither, as well by persuasion as by execution of discipline, to reform them; but little have I prevailed, for a more stiff-necked, wilful or obstinate people did I never know or hear of: doubtless they are reconciled to Rome and sworn to the Pope. . . . To some I have offered lodging and diet in my house, that I might have conference with them for their conformity; but they chose rather to go to prison."

It is at this point that we meet a large number of the Forty. Father Cuthbert Maine had been born in Devonshire. After the custom of the time he was ordained having studied in the house of his uncle, also a priest. At nineteen, following ordination, he went off to Oxford to undertake formal studies. At the outbreak of the persecution directed primarily at the clergy, Father Maine left for Douai, on the French coast, to continue his studies at the newly constructed seminary there. He fell under the watchful care of Edmund Campion while at Douai and was much impressed by him. In 1576 he returned quietly to England to begin his ministry, staying with friends in the vicinity of Exeter.

An *Account of the Life and Death of Cuthbert Maine,* written and published in 1582 by a friend of Father Maine, relates the fast end to the young ministry of this priest. Mr. Richard Greenville, the sheriff, proceeded to the house of one Mr. Tregan on the pretense of looking for a criminal recently come up from London on the run. With force he seized the young priest and after imprisonment of some six months charged him with high treason, the proof being that he had obtained from Rome a copy of the papal decree containing the absolutions for the recently celebrated holy year, that he maintained the Bishop of Rome's supremacy in matters doctrinal, and that he had said Mass within the realm of England.

The jury balked at the indictment, as there was no evidence to the charges brought against Maine save that he was in possession, at the time of his arrest, of a "small disk of wax stamped with the figure of a lamp and blessed by the Pope." Judge Manhood, nonetheless, directed the jury to find him guilty, alleging "that where plain proofs were wanting strong presumptions ought to take their place." With the jury's verdict, the sentence of death was passed. The Latin manuscript reporting his death says that on the day before his execution his jailers approached him offering pardon if he would swear upon the Bible that the Queen was the Supreme Head of the Church of England. His answer that "the queen neither ever was nor is nor ever shall be the head of the Church in England" sealed his fate. On November 30, 1577, after having been dragged through the streets of Launceston feet first, he was hanged by the neck until dead.

As Elizabeth had inherited a strange mixture of heresy and just plain confusion, it fell to her to give some form to the new religion. She found it necessary to "create" a religion that would, in the words of E. I. Watkin's book, *Roman Catholicism in England,* "ensure the only doctrine on which she insisted – that of Royal Supremacy." Her vision of the new religion was basically that reached at Edward VI's death. Watkin describes her building of the new religion in the following manner. "She retained the ecclesiastical structure of the pre-Reformation Church, in particular a hierarchy of bishops, priests and deacons. With determination and success she insisted on a minimum of ceremonial or external changes and a fixed liturgy." Her chief architect and willing aid in all this was William Cecil whose shadow falls great and large across this period of English history.

Sir William Cecil, Baron of Burleigh and Secretary of State under Elizabeth, remarked once of Edmund Campion that he was "one of the diamonds of England." Well was he so described. Campion passed early into Oxford as a don at St. John's College where he established himself with great applause as one possessed of a quick mind and broad intellect. He later travelled to Ireland stopping long enough to write a history of the nation, and then proceeded to Douai where he continued his studies for the priesthood. In 1573 he moved to Rome and was admitted to the Society of Jesus. His first commission as a Jesuit took him to Prague in the Kingdom of Bohemia where he set about teaching and writing for seven years. It was during this interval that he was ordained a priest. His reputation as a preacher spread so wide that soon Emperor Rudolf II, Emperor of the Holy Roman Empire and King of Bohemia, presented himself on many occasions to hear this "English divine who speaks God's mind."

It soon became apparent that such talents should be placed at the disposition of his own country. So in 1580, on the assignment of his religious superior, he set out for England. Campion marked his arrival in London with a sermon on the feast of SS. Peter and Paul that drew large crowds and even greater attention. Soon he was forced to take to the road and a life of hiding. In his letter to Claude Aquaviva dated November 17, 1580, he described his life and efforts at this point: "I ride about some piece of the country every day. The harvest is wonderful great. On horseback I meditate my sermon; when I come to the house, I polish it. Then I talk with such as come to speak with me, or hear their confessions. In the mornings, after Mass, I preach, they hear with exceeding greediness, and very often receive the sacraments, for the ministrations thereof we are ever well assisted by priests, whom we find in every place, whereby both the people is well served and we much eased in our charge . . . but I cannot long escape the hands of the heretics."

On July 17, 1581, he was apprehended and placed in the custody of the Sheriff of Berkshire until such time as he could be got to London. On the rack, an instrument consisting of a large frame having rollers at each end to which the limbs are fastened and between which the body is stretched, he refused to alter his convictions. One author, Bishop Challoner, relates Campion's sense of humor reminiscent of that of Thomas More. One morning after the rack his keeper asked him how his hands and feet felt. He answered, "Not ill because not at all."

On November 14, 1581, he was brought from the Tower of the King's Bench and his trial began. In a letter to the Privy Council, Campion pleaded his case:

"Whereas I have come out of Germany and Boëmeland, being sent by my superiors, and adventured myself into this noble realm, my dear country, for the glory of God and benefit of souls, I thought it like enough that, in this busy, watchful and suspicious world, I should either sooner or later be intercepted and stopped of my course. Wherefore, providing for all events, and uncertain what may become of me . . . I supposed it needful to put this writing in a readiness, desiring your good lordships to give it your reading, for to know my course. I confess that I am (albeit unworthy) a priest of the Catholic Church . . . my charge is, of free cost to preach the Gospel, to minister the Sacraments, to instruct the simple, to confute errors. I never had mind, and am strictly forbidden by our Father that sent me (the Superior General of the Jesuits) to deal in any respect with matters of State or Policy of this Realm."

The jury was impanelled on the 20th of that month and

oddly enough passed judgment that same day in time to permit the judge to render judgment of death. The day of execution was set for December 1, 1581. Mr. Everard Hanses, quoting an eye-witness of Campion's death, wrote in 1582 that at the place of execution Campion made answer to the charges brought against him. "I am a Catholic man and a priest. In that faith have I lived and in that faith do I intend to die, and if you esteem my religion treason, then I am guilty. As for any other treason, I never committed. I stand condemned for nothing but the saying of Mass, hearing confessions, preaching and such like duties and functions of priesthood." His life at the age of 42 was ended by the ax.

A. O. Meyer, the Lutheran historian and author of *England and the Catholic Church under Queen Elizabeth*, wrote that the crowd in astonishment cried when they saw Campion and his companions dragged to his death: "They laugh, they cannot fear death." To these missionaries and martyrs Meyer pays a tribute no less enthusiastic than those paid by Catholic historians:

"In no other European country at the time of the Counter-Reformation did the Catholic Church possess clergy who discharged their priestly duties with such a holy zeal as the little band that worked in England. . . . It was the heroic period of the mission. Heroism was the offspring of persecution."

Hidden and Hunted

THE harboring and protection of hunted priests in time took on almost the form of an art in England. So widespread was it that it soon became the first problem on the list of priorities of the Privy Council. In a letter to that Council the Bishop of Worcester wrote that the reform could only be carried out "if the popish and perverse priests that live in corners and are kept in gentlemen's houses and have a great estimation with the people were restrained of their liberty and put to the oath for the Queen Majesty's Supremacy."

One of the Martyrs was a Jesuit brother known as "Little John," who was himself quite expert at providing the little hiding places in which the priests took refuge when necessary. In Cambridgeshire, north of London, you can still see one of the priest holes designed by "Little John." Sawston Hall is a stately country home rising above typical English meadowlands. Part of the beauty of this estate is the tall eaved tower that dominates the inner court of the complex of buildings called the manor. Cleverly concealed under the eaves of the tower an informed eye can search out the hole that acts as a ventilation outlet for the hiding hole tucked in under the roof of the same tower. Measuring less than nine feet by three feet the hole was large enough to contain even a portly priest who might be passing through the neighborhood. If you care to climb down into the little compartment the covering can be so adjusted as to conceal the "lodger" from sight while using his body weight to fill the otherwise hollow space should someone decide to tap the boards for the telltale sound of a fake wall.

The family in possession of the estate still relate the tale of one priest who found it necessary to hide in the tower's secret "guest room" for two weeks when unexpected house guests came for a "short friendly visit." Food was provided once a day, usually in the wee hours of the morning when the guests would be asleep in the main wing. Nicholas Owen was the real name of the brother who built so many of these "hiding holes." He claimed never to have made two hiding places the same, so that if one was discovered it did not endanger the others. "His work," wrote Father John Gerard, "was the immediate occasion of saving the lives of many hundreds of persons."

Apprehended a third time, "Little John" endured the torture inflicted by Sir Robert Cecil, first Earl of Salisbury, who took to himself the questioning of this prisoner. In violation of the law, Owen was put to the torture. And the same rupture from which he suffered, that should have spared him the rack and screw, caused his death under questioning on the 2nd of March 1606. Throughout the questioning he never mentioned the location of any of his little "hiding holes." Together to jail with "Little John" went his long-time friend, Father Thomas Ganet, who was ordered hanged, drawn and quartered on June 23, 1608. His execution, attended by more than 1000 of the faithful marked the halt in such proceedings for almost a year.

From the death of Campion to the respite in 1609, eighteen others of the Forty Martyrs met their death. Of these Fathers Ralph Sherwin and Alexander Briant, who according to the Tower Journal was shackled for making himself a small wooden cross, were executed in 1581. Fathers John Paine and Luke Henry were martyred in 1582. The first Welsh martyr, Richard Gwyn, went to his death, hanged, drawn and quartered, in 1584. So great was his resolve that the crowds at his death site to no avail cried that he be allowed to die before being cut down from the gallows for the quartering. Edmund Gennings, Swithun Wells, Polydore Plasden and Eustace White perished on December 10, 1591.

Most of the maturing years of Ralph Sherwin were spent at Oxford. He was brought up at Exeter College where he was admitted as a Fellow in 1568. His attainments were in the fields of philosophy as well as ancient languages. A contemporary writing of Sherwin noted that he was "an excellent Grecian and Hebrician." However, growing militancy of the anti-Catholic administration of the University soon forced him from this school. The growing tension between the new religion and the ancient faith on the campus at Oxford did not begin the year Sherwin decided to leave. It had a history going back to Henry's first outright fight with the Church authorities. By 1559 the situation had been aggravated to such an extent that John Jewel, writing to Henry Bullinger in May of that year, notes:

"Our universities are so depressed and ruined, that at Oxford there are scarcely two individuals who think with us; and even they are so dejected and broken in spirit, that they can do nothing. . . . You would scarcely believe so much desolation could have been effected in so short a time. So that, although it would give me the greatest pleasure, under other circumstances, to see even a dog from Zurich in England, yet I cannot at this time recommend you to send your young men to us, either for learned or religious education, unless you would have them sent back to you wicked and barbarous."

This rejection of the ancient faith at Oxford was all the more tragic given the history of its foundations. Its beginnings as a college system dated from 1240, but Marwell Fraser notes that there are traces of a Saxon nunnery and school at Oxford founded by St. Frideswide, daughter of an eighth-century Mercian king. It grew as a limited center of Christian education until it received its first royal charter as a university in 1249. Following decades witnessed the foundation of Balliol, Merton and Exeter Colleges as part of the university system. Sherwin's college, Exeter, was founded in 1314 while Clement V was busy obtaining a peace treaty between England and her regular enemy France. Today, in a building that houses part of the great Bodleian Library, one can still see part of the old Examination Schools, built in 1439, in which Sherwin would have passed his exams. The Bodleian was originally founded in the 14th century by Thomas Cobham, Bishop of Worcester, but the valuable collection of books and manuscripts was dispersed by the commissioners of Edward VI on account of their "popish" tendencies.

In the year prior to Sherwin's departure, another step was taken to drive out the Catholic traditions of this institution. On May 5, 1573, the queen's commissioners, Lawrence Humfrey, Herbert Westfaling, Joseph Kennall and William Cole, addressed this stern message to the Fellows of Magdalen College:

"Whereas by credible report we are informed that as yet there are remaining in your college diverse monuments of superstition undefaced . . . (we) will and command you forthwith upon the sight hereof utterly to deface, or cause to be defaced, so that they may not hereafter serve to any superstitious purpose, all copes, vestments, albs, missals, books, crosses and such other idolatrous monuments whatsoever, and within eight days after the receipt hereof to bring true certificate of their whole doing herein to us our colleagues, whereof fail you not as you will answer to the contrary at your peril."

Not everyone, particularly among the student body, went along with these drastic, iconaclast changes. The *History and Antiquities of the University of Oxford* relates how students objected forcefully to the suppression of their religion and the negation of their religious services. Unfortunately, notes the same work, these protests were brought to speedy conclusion by appropriate force.

Sherwin, after leaving Oxford, travelled to France and

the Seminary at Douai. After completing his studies in March 1577 he was ordained by the Bishop of Cambray. From that year until 1580 he continued studies in Rome. With his education behind him the new priest left the Continent for England. Originally he had planned to accompany Dr. Goldwell, Bishop of St. Asaph, on a confirmation tour before actually starting on his own mission. However, the illness of his friend, the bishop, compelled Sherwin to begin his England ministry alone.

The priestly ministry of Ralph Sherwin was cut short by his arrest, imprisonment, trial and condemnation. He summed up his state of soul and mind in a letter to his uncle, the Reverend John Woodward, the night before his execution:

"My Dearest Uncle,

"After many conflicts, mixed with spiritual consolations and Christian comforts, it hath pleased God, of His infinite mercy, to call me out of this vale of misery. To Him, therefore, for all His benefit, all times and for ever be praise and glory.

". . .

"This very morning, which is the festival of St. Andrew, I was advertised by superior authority that tomorrow I was to end the course of this life. God grant that I may do it to the imitation of his noble apostles . . .

"Innocency is my only comfort against all the forged villainy which is gathered on my fellow priests and me. Well, then by the High Judge, God Himself, this false vizard of treason shall be removed from true Catholic men's faces . . .

"Prayers for my soul procure me . . . farewell,

Your Cousin,
Ralph Sherwin, Priest."

On the morning of his execution Sherwin was asked his opinion on the Bull of Pope Pius. He remained silent. Then asked if he were willing to pray for the queen, he replied, "I have and do." At which words writes Bishop Challoner, "Lord Howard again asked which queen he meant, whether it be Elizabeth Queen? To whom, somewhat smiling, he (Sherwin) said, 'Yea for Elizabeth Queen I now at this instant pray my Lord God to make her His servant in this life, and after this life coheir with Jesus Christ." Thus ended Ralph Sherwin, protesting adherence to both his queen and his Church.

From the excommunication of Henry VIII by Clement VII until the time of Sherwin a great change had taken place in English political structure and life. Ecclesiastical authority was broken and the life-giving tie with Rome severed. Part of the story of the great rupture includes the bull, *Regnans in Excelsis,* of Pius V. In a strongly worded decree this Pope not only excommunicated Elizabeth, who really felt no tie with the Church in any case, but also "deposed her" insofar as it absolved her subjects from allegiance to her. There were, and continue to be, many reactions to this action. In a letter to Geran de Spes in the same year as the publication of the bull, Philip II, King of Spain and the recognized "strong man" of Europe, explained his reaction: "His Holiness (Pius V) has taken this step without communicating with me in any way, which has surprised me, because my knowledge of English affairs is such that I believe I could give a better opinion on them and the course that ought to have been adopted . . . than anyone else.

"Since, however, His Holiness, no doubt thought what he did was the only thing requisite for all to turn out as he wished, and if such were the case, I of all the faithful sons of the Holy See, would rejoice the most. But I fear that not only this will not be the case, but that this sudden and unexpected step will exacerbate things there and drive the Queen and her friends the more to oppress and persecute the few good Catholics remaining in England."

Philip, Son of Emperor Charles V, brother of the then ruling Holy Roman Emperor, who, as king of Spain, held dominion over half of Italy, the Netherlands, part of France, Portugal and most of the Americas, north and south, did not, interestingly enough, question the authority of the Pope to restrict or even depose a monarch in pursuit of the salvation of the true and ancient faith. In fact, given the history up to that date and the general suppositions held by most at that time, he could only accept the ruling of the "head of Christendom." His critique is limited solely to whether or not such a ruling will have its effect—will it work?

Elizabeth, having rejected the Church with the ancient faith, felt no compunction in disregarding the new ruling. She had in fact set aside the ruling of her own father, Henry VIII, and the Parliament of England, which had declared her illegitimate and "unfit" to rule. She intended to consolidate her reign and the bull was but one more effectual hindrance.

None of the Martyrs listed among the Forty felt obliged to choose between their Queen and the Church. The documents concerning the death of all the Forty show that the terms of the imprisonment and execution were clear. The choice was between the new religion and the ancient faith. A typical reply of the Forty is found in a letter written by Father John Paine. Paine was born in Northamptonshire and was educated in England, then at Douai. In 1576 he was ordained priest and returned to England where he worked mainly in Essex until he was apprehended in 1581. Before his execution, he penned his position, directing it to the Lieutenant of the Tower, Mr. Eliot:

"My duty remembered, being not able to write without better hands (this was after his punishment on the racks), I have by your appointment used the help of your servant. For answer unto your interrogations, I have already said sufficient for a man that regardeth his own salvation, and that with such advised asseverations uttered as amongst Christian men ought to be believed, yet once again briefly for obedience sake.

"First, touching her Majesty, I pray God long to preserve her Highness to His honor and her heart's desire: unto whom I always have, and during life will wish, no worse than to my own soul. If her pleasure be not that I shall live and serve her as my sovereign prince, then will I willingly die her faithful subject, and, I trust, God's true servant.

"Touching the State, I protest that I am, and ever have been, free from the knowledge of any practice whatsoever, either within or without the realm, intended against the same; for the verity whereof, as I have often before you and the rest of her Grace's commissioners called God to witness, so do I now again; and one day before His Majesty the truth now not credited will then be revealed.

"For Eliot, I forgive his monstrous wickedness, and defy his malicious inventions; wishing that his former behaviour toward others, being well known, as hereafter it will, were not a sufficient disproof of these devised slanders.

"For . . . other persons living in London . . . I answer at my utmost peril to the charge of being a priest and a Catholic.

"Her Majesty's faithful subject, and Your Worship's humble prisoner,

John Paine, Priest."

Challoner notes that "Paine's execution is recorded by Mr. Stow in his Annals, 1582–John Paine, priest, being indicted of high treason, for words by him spoken to one Eliot, was arraigned, condemned, and executed at Chelmsford." Strange were the events that prepared for and lead up to the ever stranger situation that prevailed at the time of Paine's death. The queen of England claimed to be Head of the Church in England while the Pope claimed to exercise political authority in Christendom.

Outlaw Catholics

ON to the scene came another of the Forty, Luke Kirby, priest. According to Allen's *Brief History* Kirby was born in Richmond in Yorkshire. His studies were completed at the English College in Rome and he returned via Switzerland in the company of Campion and Sherwin. With a certain sense of adventure, he challenged Beza, the Calvinist scholar, to a debate on the new religion versus the ancient faith. His wager was that the loser face death. The challenge went without a taker even in Geneva.

Immediately on his return to England he was arrested. The question of the bull *Regnans in excelsis* was brought up as well as the more important question, "Who speaks for the Church and, therefore, for God—the Queen or the Vicar of Christ?" To the first question Kirby replied, "That the excommunication by Pius V was a matter of fact, wherein the Pope might err, the which I do leave to himself to answer for."

"Notwithstanding," he continued, "I do acknowledge to my queen as much duty and authority as ever I did to Queen Mary, or as any subject in France, Spain, or Italy doth acknowledge to his King or Prince . . . and more with safety of conscience I cannot do." For Kirby the matter was clearly one of conscience, not politics, not intrigue, least of all treason, but of conscience, simple and clear. The

Pope could declare himself in exercise of political power in Europe, the queen could declare herself Head of the Church in England; Kirby was prepared to dispute both. For the rejection of the latter he was to face the "Scavenger's Daughter" and death.

The "Tower Journal" lists the "Scavenger's Daughter" as an instrument of torture that "consists of an iron ring which brings the head, feet and hands together until they form a circle." The same journal notes that on "10 October 1584, Luke Kirby, priest, suffered compression on the Scavenger's Daughter for more than an hour." He was executed 15 October 1584.

By the time Edmund Gennings was born at Lichfield in Staffordshire in 1567 there existed in England, in fact, two religions, one enjoying the patronage and protection of the State, the other outlawed. It was in the former that Edmund was baptized and came of age. Following the custom of the time, he entered the service of another family, a member of the gentry, at the age of 16. The Sherwoods were Catholics. And while in the service of this family, Edmund converted to the Catholic faith. When the young Sherwood announced that he intended to go to Douai to study for the priesthood, Gennings followed his example. In 1589, as an ordained priest, Edmund returned to England to take up the office as a "roving priest." By this time the remnants of his family were dead except his brother John who, after moving to London, had become bitterly anti-Catholic. Edmund went in search of his brother and also ended up in London sometime in 1591. Clement Tigar, in his short work in *Forty Martyrs of England and Wales*, relates the incidents connected with the arrest of Father Gennings:

"He made arrangements to say Mass in Gray's Inn Fields at the house of Mr. Swithun Wells on November 7, 1591, and told a few Catholics of the rendezvous. Very early in the morning, a little group of Catholics made their way to the house, and Father Gennings commenced the Mass in an upper room. Just as he reached the consecration there was a loud banging on the front door below. When the door was opened, Topcliffe, with other officers, broke in and rushed upstairs. One of the gentlemen assisting at Mass thought it best under circumstances to hurl Topcliffe downstairs, and he did so. In a few minutes Topcliffe came upstairs again, his head all bleeding, and tried to break into the room where Mass was in progress, but the gentlemen present kept him out. Fearing he might raise the whole street, they said if he would wait till the end of Mass they would surrender, but if he attempted to profane the sacred mysteries, they would be obliged to oppose force by force. Topcliffe accepted the terms and Father Gennings continued the Mass to the end, the Catholic gentlemen present standing with drawn swords. When Mass was over, they surrendered, and Topcliffe rushed in and seized Father Gennings before he had time to unvest. All present, to the number of about ten, were arrested and taken to Newgate."

The evidence presented at the trial was that Father Gennings had said Mass. Apparently this was all that was needed to convict him and off he went to the gallows. Ten days afterwards, the Martyr's brother, John was received into the Church, went to Douai, was ordained a priest and later became a Franciscan monk.

By the late 16th and early 17th centuries the sporadic and impulsive arrests and executions of priests reached a new high. E. I. Watkin notes that after 1585 the majority of condemnations were made simply for being priests in England. But still the tide was not stemmed. By 1585, 229 priests came to England from Douai, and 33 were sent from the Venerable English College in Rome. Of these 70 were imprisoned and 23 were put to death within a year of their arrival. Sometimes, however, loyalties went against the official position even in those charged to implement the royal laws. Some jailers winked at the saying of Mass by the prisoners and Watkin maintains that "the prisons, in fact, became centers of Catholic ministry, to some extent even of propaganda, where a priest could be found to do his office."

Richard Vaughan, the Bishop of Chester, wrote on January 29, 1598, to his friend, Thomas Hesketh, complaining of the rather lax attitude taken by some jailers in the face of their Catholic prisoners:

"I hear that the prison at Lancaster is very ill kept; that recusants there have liberty to go when and whither they list; to hunt, hawk, and go to horse races; which notorious abuse of law and justice should be speedily reformed."

Archbishop Whitgift received a somewhat indignant letter from the Privy Council complaining of "the great hurt the priests do in saying Mass in those prisons and the company that resort unto them, which by that means are made in a manner so many seminaries." The government policy indicated in that same letter boiled down to the instruction to deport those priests not held for execution.

The overwhelming number of priests coming into England were Englishmen sent abroad and trained at the College of Douai in France. But the next largest source of priests for the English isle was the Venerable English College in Rome. The students in both these institutions were in part supported by the Holy Father's contributions and in part by what English Catholics could smuggle out of England in the way of funds. Most times the antics attempted to get funds to the continent seem to resemble those employed in the 1960's by Englishmen avoiding the "ceiling" then placed on funds taken out of the country by would-be tourists. In a letter to the king of Spain, dated May 6, 1583, Bernardino de Mendoza, Ambassador to the Court of Queen Elizabeth, wrote:

"The Queen maintains such a multitude of spies in France to dog the footsteps of the English Catholics there, that it is not possible for their friends to send them a penny without her hearing of it. They therefore constantly have recourse to me, and I send the money as if it were my own. I have now 10,000 crowns which they have asked me to send."

The smuggling in of the priests trained in France and Rome gave rise to many an adventure as well as proud boast. In a letter to Father John Agazarri in Rome an English port official bragged of his part in the operation. William Allen wrote, dated 23 June, 1581: "Thirty priests at least have entered England since Easter, nor was any one of them hindered at this port, or afterwards taken, blessed be God!"

Deuincti ad carros, perque urbis compita ducti,
Libera seruili lacerantur terga flagello.
Supplicio hoc functis, mox tanq̃ erronibus aures
Perfossæ, igniti terebrantur acumine ferri. 3

Victim flogged; interrogations in the foreground.

Women and Nobility

NOT all of these martyrs were priests, indeed, not all men. Among the women number Ann Line, Margaret Ward and Margaret Clitherow. The latter Margaret was brought up a Protestant and married a lapsed Catholic who was by trade a butcher. However, in 1574 Margaret converted and entered into active collaboration with the priests who were returning from Douai. In 1586, after Mass has been said in the makeshift school she ran for Catholic children, she was arrested. Eventually one of the young schoolchildren was forced by the arresting officers to show where the Mass articles were kept hidden. Mary Claridge, in her book *Margaret Clitherow*, relates the following: In court Margaret refused to plead so that she "might not bring others into danger by her conviction or be an accessory to the juryman's sins in condemning the innocent." Her death was a particularly barbaric one. It was decreed that she be pressed to death.

John Mush in his *Life of Margaret Clitherow* describes her death.

"The women took off her clothes, and put upon her the long habit of linen. A door was laid upon her, her hands bound to two posts so that her body and arms made a cross. After this they laid weight upon her, which when she first felt, she said, 'Jesus, Jesus, have mercy on me!'

which were the last words she was heard to speak. She was in dying one quarter of an hour. A sharp stone, as much as a man's fist, was put under her back; upon her was laid to the quantity of seven or eight hundredweight at the least, which, breaking her ribs, caused them to burst forth of the skin."

Margaret Ward's story began when first she heard of the imprisonment of Father Watson. She obtained leave of the lady for whom she worked and made a visit to the neglected priest. Through her friendship with the jailer's wife, she eventually got permission to see Father Watson from time to time and bring him certain necessities. The conditions set for her visits were that she be searched at each visit and neither carry in nor out any letters. At length Margaret learned from Father Watson that if he had some rope he could let himself down from one of the unwatched rooms and escape. Mrs. Ward procured the rope and in the *History of Margaret Ward,* from Dr. Champney's manuscript, the following tale unravels along with the cord.

She brought to the prison in her basket under cover of bread and vegetables the needed cord. Being by this time a familiar face, she went in freely, the guard neglecting to search either her or the basket. After due time she left the prison and notified two Catholic watermen to keep their boat near Bridwell, the prison, between two and three in the morning, at which time the planned escape would take place.

Father Watson, planning on taking with him the rope, doubled it around the bars rather than tying it to them. In this manner he would leave no clue as to how he got away. The rope folded this way turned out to be much too short to allow him to reach the bottom. After some indecision he chanced a fall that broke both his right arm and leg. The rope remained behind as the two shoremen dragged off the unconscious priest to their boat. The next day Mrs. Ward was arrested and after eight days was brought to court. The sentence was death.

On August 30, 1588, after refusing a complete full pardon in return for attendance at the services of the new church, she was executed. Within the year Father Watson was again apprehended and, rejecting the same choice that had been offered Margaret Ward, was duly dispatched by the hangman.

Ann Line, as her biographers describe her, was a sickly woman troubled with continual headaches and dropsy. This condition did not seem either to dampen her spirits or slow her activities. Like Margaret Clitherow, she provided space and opportunities for priests to offer Mass as they passed through her neighborhood. On Candlemas Day, 1601, she got caught. While a Father Page was saying Mass a group of officials attempted to break into her house. However, the bolt held long enough for Father Page to unvest and escape. On the evidence of a fellow who claimed he saw a man dressed in white near her house on the day of the crime, Ann Line was convicted. Her infirmities haunted her even to the scaffold. So weak and ill was she that she had to be carried to Tyburn for the execution. Having dismissed the ministers proffered her by the local officials, she addressed the crowd, letting at least them know that she felt no contrition for the action that had led to this unhappy end. "I am sentenced to die for harboring a Catholic priest, and so far am I from repenting for having so done that I wish, with all my soul, that where I have entertained one, I could have entertained one thousand." Thus ended the mortal days of Mrs. Line.

Of the nobility there is represented among the Forty Martyrs, Philip Howard, Earl of Arundel and Surrey, the son and heir of the Duke of Norfolk. Although raised a Protestant he was received into the Church in 1584. At this time he prepared to leave England in voluntary exile. His plan called for him to leave a letter for the queen to be delivered after his departure, telling that, "for his soul's health and the service of God" he planned to leave his native country but not his loyal affection for Her Majesty. One of his servants betrayed him as he went on board the ship. He passed the next ten years in jail at the bidding of the

Star Chamber. In the middle cell of the Beauchamp Tower of the Tower of London one can still see the inscription on the wall over the fireplace: "Quante plus afflictionis pro Christo in hoc saeculo, tanto plus gloriae in futuro: Arundell 1587." (The more suffering for Christ in this life, the more glory in the life to come.)

Not all of Howard's life had been equally pious. When he went to court at the age of 18 he was handsome, intelligent and the toast of many a party. Enjoying the queen's favor, he soon let himself become captive of the glamor of the court life. Flattered by the queen's attention, he led what would most kindly be described as a "worldly" life. One day, when he was 24 and at the height of his prowess and fame at court, he visited the Tower to hear a debate between Edmund Campion, its most noted occupant at the time, and some theologians of the new religion. Apparently impressed by what he heard, he left both the Tower and the life at court, retiring to his wife and family castle at Arundel. Three years later he was received into the Church in London by the Jesuit priest, William Watson.

Lord Howard did not tell his wife of the reason for the visit to London and she, not knowing of his plans, used the time of his absence to seek out an old Marian priest who received her into the Church at Arundel. It was shortly after this period that they planned the abortive trip to France which ended in his permanent residency in the Tower. Eventually, after repeatedly refusing his liberty in return for an appearance in a Protestant church, he died emaciated, though most reports say poisoned, in 1595. That year saw the execution of Henry Walpole who endured the rack more than a dozen times. Robert Southwell met death that same year, before a huge and reverent crowd at Tyburn. Before the turn of the century three more of the Forty met their death: John Jones, a priest who obtained his permission to return to England from Pope Clement VIII personally; John Rigby, a man servant in the household of Sir Edmund Huddleston, a Protestant member of the minor nobility; and John Boste, a secular priest of Westmorland.

The humor of many of the martyrs is recorded alongside their deeds as testimony to the Christian joy with which they faced both life and death. John Roberts, a lawyer who was converted to the faith while travelling in Paris, was arrested at Mass upon his return to England. On the scaffold as they prepared a fire with which to heat the irons for his quartering, he remarked: "I see you prepare a hot breakfast for us."

In 1603, Elizabeth I passed before the judgment seat of God. In the Diary of John Manningham he notes, "This morning about three o'clock Her Majesty departed this life, mildly like a lamb, easily like a ripe apple from a tree." She was succeeded by James of the House of Stuart.

Vt. quibus excepti domibus myſteria Chriſti
Egerunt. quòsque à funeſtro ſchiſmate ſanctæ
Iunxere Ecclesiæ, pródant, et talia multa
Diſtendunt miseros diris cruciatibus artus

Captive on rack; others forced to hear his cries.

Martyrs of Elizabeth's Successors

KING JAMES was the son of Mary Stuart and hailed already as James VI of Scotland. With his ascension to the throne of England on March 24, 1603, he became James I, King of both England and Scotland. The Scots had brought him up in the Protestant faith and his preference was for a united realm—united in one church. As a supporter of the theory of the divine right of kings to rule, he insisted that the faith, or at least the church, be one and united behind him as God's regent on earth for the British Isles.

John Almond challenged the right of James to impose his religion on the people as a matter of public policy. It is possible to be a Catholic and at the same time a loyal subject of the crown was his position. For it, he was to pay dearly. Almond's service in the Church began at about his 15th or 16th year as he left his home in Allerton, Lancashire, to attend school at Much-Wooton not too far from Liverpool. His studies carried him abroad and he eventually passed through Douai College on his way to the English College in Rome. Not much is heard of him upon his return to England until his arrest in 1612. A rather long account of his trial is found in Bishop Challoner's book, *Memoirs of Missionary Priests.* The point upon which he based his defense was a simple one: a person can be at the same time a loyal Englishman and a faithful Catholic. There exists no reason why the thesis cannot be sustained and upon its defense Almond risked his life. Religion and the rights of free exercise of conscience in the face of a religious conviction do not necessarily compromise one's loyalty to the order of the realm. Much less so does the voice of religious conviction automatically reek of treason. Dr. King, Bishop of London, recorded the hearing at which Almond protested: "I do bear in my heart and soul all the allegiance to King James as he or any Christian King could expect by the laws of nature, and the law of God or the positive law of the true Church." That same year he was hanged, drawn and quartered.

Another graduate of the English College followed this same ill-fated line of defense before the king's bench some years later. The speech he made from the gallows confirmed the position that one can be both Catholic, even a priest, and English. Pope Paul, in the canonization ceremony, October 25, 1970, in St. Peter's Basilica before more than 30,000 witnesses—over half of whom had come from England—repeated the final plea of John Plessington:

"Bear witness, good hearers, that I profess that I undoubtedly and firmly believe all the articles of the Roman Catholic faith, and for the truth of any of them, by the assistance of God, I am willing to die; and I had rather die than doubt of any point of faith taught by our holy Mother the Roman Catholic Church . . . God bless the King and the royal family and grant His Majesty a prosperous reign here, and a crown of glory hereafter. God grant peace to the subjects and that they live and die in true faith, hope and charity. That which remains is that I recommend my self to the mercy of Jesus, by whose merits I hope for mercy. O Jesus, be to me a Jesus."

James I was followed on the throne in 1625 by Charles I, but Catholics fared no better under him. Of the Forty Martyrs, Alban Roe, a Benedictine priest, and Henry Morse, a Jesuit, both saw the gallows and the quarterers' irons. Father Morse was a man who, even without the tale of events that led to his martyrdom, could quality for canonization. He fits into the pattern of "a plague priest" familiar enough to readers of European history. The year 1636 saw a terrible plague strike London. Some sections of the city seemed harder hit than others and the area around St. Giles-in-the-Fields ranked near the top as a disaster area. One report lists a deathrate reaching over 4,000 a month for the city with the St. Giles area well near the top in contributions to this grim roll call.

Within the context of this plague and the locality of St. Giles the life of Father Henry Morse first comes to the attention of biographers. He spent a great deal of time visiting the homes of the stricken to bring both the comfort of what physical kind he could and the consolations of the Church reserved to those soon to leave this world. Clement Tigar relates that Father Morse once himself fell victim to the plague but soon was well enough to resume his charitable work. Arrested once on charges of being a priest, he was released after an imprisonment at Newgate. His adventurous nature seems to have involved him in many a ministry, for we read of his pastoral works in Cornwall, his retreats preached for soldiers during his banishment at Ghent and his work with the Sisters at Antwerp just prior to his return to England.

Not too long after his arrival he was apprehended on suspicion of being a priest. Since he had been tried once on this charge and found guilty there was no need, in the mind of his judge, to repeat the whole affair. He was ordered dispatched on the 1st of February, 1645.

But things were not going so well for the king, either. Factions were everywhere dividing the loyalties of too many subjects. Enough people were now whispering quite loudly that perhaps England were better off without a king. Unable to control his heritage, Charles granted religious liberty to the Presbyterians in Scotland, hoping vainly to win a respite for himself in what was shaping up as a civil war in England. The Puritan faction under Oliver Cromwell was now a force to be reckoned with. In 1649, Charles, after repeated military defeats, was imprisoned, forced to abdicate, and was eventually beheaded at Whitehall on January 30.

For the first time in the annals of English history, since 827 when Egbert, King of Wessex was declared King of the English, there was no longer a king. The Commonwealth was declared, and Cromwell named Protector. Now the persecution of the Church reached new heights. John Southwell fell in 1654 in the first year of the newly proclaimed Protectorate. So steadfast and good had he been that even his judge, while imposing the sentence of death, wept. On the scaffold he addressed the huge crowd which had gathered in spite of the rain: "My faith and obedience to my superiors is all the treason charged against me; may I die for Christ's law, which no human law, by whomsoever made, ought to withstand or contradict. This Church, these superiors of it, I obeyed, and for obeying, die. I was brought up in the truly ancient Roman Catholic apostolic religion, which taught me the sum of the only true Christian profession is to die."

Southwell left behind him in the prison cell of the Tower a smattering of verse and poems that he had compiled to while away the long silent hours. After his death these various writings were collected and published as religious poetry. The popularity of his style claims as a witness the fact that his works went through 11 editions beginning with the first which came out within the same year as his death.

In 1658 Oliver Cromwell died, succeeded by the inept Richard Cromwell. By May of that same year he had resigned as Lord Protector. On May 1, 1660, Charles II was proclaimed king, thus restoring a somewhat tarnished but nonetheless viable monarchy. He entered London to be hailed King of England of May 29, 1660. Under him, Philip Evans and John Lloyd were martyred outside Cardiff Castle on July 22, 1679. Both were priests. Within this reign the remaining Forty Martyrs—John Plessington, secular priest; John Wall, Franciscan Father; John Kemble and David Lewis, Jesuit priests—were executed for the faith.

John Kemble, so relates the Diary of Douai College,

was born in Hereford. In February 1625 he was ordained a priest, said his first Mass and set out for England, arriving June 5th the same year. His life span reached 80 years, reminiscent of Psalm 89, of which 54 years were spent in the ministry of the priesthood. On August 22, 1679, the news came to him in his prison shackles that he was to face death that day. He asked but three things: the time to say his prayers, smoke his pipe and drink a cup of sack. Unfortunately his executioner was not so calm and Father Kemble, aged 80, hung for one half an hour before he died. The quartering, now so much a part of the treatment afforded Catholic priests in England, was delayed as no one dared carry out so revolting a sentence on this man. His dissection mercifully followed his death.

Postscript

ON Monday, May 18, 1970, Pope Paul VI presided at a Consistory of the College of Cardinals at which the final decision was made to canonize the Forty Martyrs of England and Wales. The press statement issued in London that day reads, in part, as follows:

"In penal times in England, Protestants and Catholics died at the hands of governments who favored their respective religions. Both died, however, for what they respectively held as the true Christian faith. It is this common factor which the modern ecumenical movement tries to emphasise. Today the emphasis is laid, not on the dispute leading to the martyrdom, but on the prayer repeated by one martyr after another on the scaffold for England and the Church, that they and witnesses to their death would soon meet again in heaven."

Before a crowd swelled by the presence of over 14,000 English and Welsh men and women, Pope Paul VI canonized and recognized for public veneration the Forty English Martyrs, stating that they are in fact friends of God and with Him today. The papal bull so proclaiming them recalls their heroic virtue. The Pope's remarks made application to this day of the lesson taught in the lives and actions of the Forty.

"The solemn canonization of the Forty Martyrs of England and Wales that we have just carried out, gives us the welcome opportunity to speak to you, though briefly, on the significance of their existence, and on the importance that their lives and their deaths have had and continue to have not only for the Church in England and Wales but also for the Universal Church, for each of us and for every man of goodwill.

"Our times need Saints, and particularly the example of those who gave the supreme testimony of their love for Christ and His Church. 'Greater love has no man than this, that a man lay down his life for his friends' (Jn. 15, 13). These words of the Divine Master, which refer in the first instance to the sacrifice that He himself made on the cross, offering himself for the salvation of the whole of mankind, can also be applied to the great and elect host of martyrs of all times, from the first persecution of the newborn Church to those of our days, perhaps less overt, but equally cruel."

"A great deal has been said and written about that mysterious being, man: about the resources of his intellect, capable of penetrating the secrets of the universe and of subjugating material things, utilizing them for his own purposes; about the grandeur of the human spirit, manifested in the admirable works of science and art; about his nobility and his weakness; his triumphs and his wretchedness. But that which characterizes man, that which is the most intimate element in his being and his personality, is the capacity to love, to love to the end, to give himself with that love that is stronger than death and extends into eternity.

"The martyrdom of Christians is the most sublime expression and sign of this love, not only because the martyr remains faithful to his love to the extent of shedding his blood, but also because this sacrifice is performed out of the loftiest and noblest love that can exist, namely love for Him who created and redeemed us, who loves us as only He can love, and expects from us a response of total and unconditioned giving, that is, a love worthy of our God."

Canonization Homily of Pope Paul VI

THE solemn canonization of the forty martyrs of England and Wales that we have just carried out gives us the welcome opportunity to speak to you, though briefly, on the significance of their existence, and on the importance that their lives and their deaths have had and continue to have not only for the Church in England and Wales but also for the Universal Church, for each of us and for every man of goodwill.

Our times need saints, and particularly the example of those who gave the supreme testimony of their lives for Christ and His Church. "Greater love has no man than this, that a man lay down his life for his friends" (Jn. 15, 13). These words of the Divine Master, which refer in the first instance to the sacrifice that He Himself made on the cross, offering Himself for the salvation of the whole of mankind, can also be applied to the great and elect host of martyrs of all times, from the first persecution of the new-born Church to those of our days, perhaps less overt, but equally cruel.

The Church of Christ was born from the sacrifice of Christ on the cross and she continues to grow and develop in virtue of the heroic love of her most authentic sons and daughters. "Semen est sanguis Christianorum" (Blood is the seed of Christians). Like the shedding of Christ's blood, so the martyrs' oblation of their lives becomes in virtue of their union with Christ's sacrifice a source of life and spiritual fertility for the Church and for the whole world.

"By martyrdom a disciple is transformed into an image of his Master, who freely accepted death on behalf of the world's salvation. He perfects that image even to the shedding of blood. The Church, therefore, considers martyrdom as an exceptional gift and as the highest proof of love," the constitution *Lumen Gentium* (No. 42) reminds us.

A great deal has been said and written about that mysterious being, man: about the resources of his intellect, capable of penetrating the secrets of the universe and of subjugating material things, utilizing them for his own purposes; about the grandeur of the human spirit, manifested in the admirable works of science and art; about his nobility and his weaknesses. But what characterizes man, what is the most intimate element in his being and his personality, is the capacity to love to the end, to give himself with that love that is stronger than death and extends into eternity.

The martyrdom of Christians is the most sublime expression and sign of this love, not only because the martyr remains faithful to his love to the extent of shedding his blood, but also because this sacrifice is performed out of the loftiest and noblest love that can exist, namely love for Him who created and redeemed us, and expects from us a response of total and unconditional giving, that is, a love worthy of our God.

In its long and glorious history, Great Britain, island of saints, has given to the world many men and women who loved God with this sincere, loyal love. For this reason we are glad to have been able today to number forty other sons and daughters of this noble land among those that the Church publicly recognizes as saints. By so doing she proposes them to the veneration of her faithful in order that the latter may draw a vivid example from their lives.

To anyone who reads, moved and admiring, the records of their martyrdom, it is clear—we should like to say evident—that they are worthy emulators of the greatest martyrs of the past, owing to the great humility, fearlessness, simplicity and serenity with which they accepted their sentence and their death, nay even more, with spiritual joy and an admirable and radiant charity.

It is just this deep, spiritual attitude that brackets together and unites these men and women, who in other respects differed from one another in everything that can distinguish such a large group of persons, that is, age and sex, culture and education, state and social condition of life, character and temperament, natural and supernatural dispositions, the external circumstances of their existence. Among the forty holy martyrs we have, in fact, secular and Religious priests, Religious of various orders and of different rank. We have laymen of noble birth and of humble origins. We have women who were married and mothers of a family. What unites all of them is that spiritual attitude of unshakable loyalty to the call of God which asked them, as a response of love, for the sacrifice of their lives.

And the martyrs' response was unanimous. "I cannot forbear to tell you again that I die for God and religion's sake," St. Philip Evans said, "and I find myself so happy that if I ever could have several other lives I would be disposed to sacrifice them all for so noble a cause."

And, like many others, St. Philip Howard, Earl of Arundel, asserted, "I am sorry I have only one life to offer for this noble cause." And St. Margaret Clitherow, with moving simplicity, summed up the meaning of her life and death: "I am dying for love of my Lord Jesus."

"What a little thing this is, if compared with the far crueller death that Christ suffered for me," exclaimed St. Alban Roe.

Like many of their fellow countrymen who died in similar circumstances, these forty men and women of England and Wales wanted to be, and were until the end, loyal to their country which they loved with all their heart. They wanted to be, and were, faithful subjects of the crown which they all – without any exception – recognized up to the moment of their death as the legitimate authority in everything pertaining to civil and political matters.

But this was the drama of the lives of these martyrs, namely, that their honest and sincere loyalty to the civil authority came into conflict with loyalty to God and with what, according to the dictates of their conscience illuminated by Catholics faith, they knew involved revealed truths, especially on the Holy Eucharist and on the inalienable prerogatives of Peter's successor who is, by God's will, the universal pastor of the Church of Christ.

Placed before the choice of remaining faithful to their faith and therefore dying for it, or saving their lives by denying their faith, they rallied to God without a moment's hesitation and with a really supernatural strength, and joyfully faced martyrdom. But so great was their spirit, so noble were their sentiments, so Christian was the inspiration of their lives, that many of them died praying for their beloved country, for the king or for the queen, and even for those who had been directly responsible for their capture, tortures and the ignominous circumstances of their cruel death.

The last words and the last prayer of St. John Plessington were, in fact, these: "God bless the king and the royal family and grant His Majesty a prosperous reign here, and a crown of glory hereafter. God grant peace to the subjects of the king and allow them to live and die in true faith, hope, and charity."

Thus St. Alban Roe, just before he was hanged, prayed: "Forgive me, my God, my countless offenses, as I forgive my persecutors." Similarly, St. Thomas Garnet, after naming individually and forgiving those who had betrayed, arrested and condemned him, besought God: "May all attain salvation and with me reach heaven."

On reading the records of their martyrdom and meditating on the rich material collected so carefully on the historical circumstances of their lives and their martyrdom, we are struck above all by that which shines forth unmistakably and luminously in their lives. There is an element that by its very nature is such as to transcend the centuries, and is always fully relevant and of vital importance, particularly in our days.

We are referring to the fact that these heroic sons and daughters of England and Wales took their faith really seriously. This means that they accepted it as the only norm of life and of their whole conduct, a norm from which they received great serenity and deep spiritual joy. With a freshness and spontaneity not lacking in humor, that precious gift characteristic of their people, with an attachment to their duty averse from all ostentation, and with the sincerity typical of those who live with deep and well-rooted convictions, these martyr saints are a radiant example of the Christian who really lives his baptismal consecration, and grows in that life that was given to him in the sacrament of initiation and strength in that of Confirmation. In this way religion is not a marginal factor for him, but the very essence of all his being and acting, so that divine charity becomes the inspiring, active and operating force of an existence straining towards the union of love with God and with all men of goodwill, which will finds its fullness in eternity.

The Church and the world of today greatly need such men and women, from all walks of life, priests, Religious and laymen. Only persons of such stature and such holiness will be able to change our tormented world and restore to it, together with peace, that spiritual and truly Christian orientation for which every man longs at heart—even sometimes without being aware of it—and which we all need so much.

May our gratitude rise to God for having, in his providential goodness, raised up these holy martyrs. Their industry and sacrifice have contributed to the preservation of the Catholic faith in England and Wales.

May the Lord continue to raise up in the Church laymen, Religious and priests who are worthy emulators of these heralds of the faith.

May God grant, in His love, that centers of study, formation and prayer may flourish and develop today, too, to prepare, in today's conditions, holy priests and missionaries. Such were, in those times, the venerable and the glorious seminaries of St. Omer and Douai, from the ranks of which many of the forty martyrs came. One of them, a great personality, St. Edmund Campion, said, "This Church will never weaken as long as there are priests and pastors to attend to their flock."

May the Lord grant us the grace that, in these times of growing religious indifferentism and theoretical and practical materialism, the example and intercession of the forty holy martyrs may encourage us in faith and strengthen our authentic love for God, for His Church and for all men.

May the blood of these martyrs be able to heal the great wound inflicted upon God's Church by reason of the separation of the Anglican Church from the Catholic Church.

Is it not one—these martyrs say to us—the Church founded by Christ? Is not this their witness? Their devotion to their nation gives us the assurance that on the day when—God willing—the unity of the faith and of Christian life is restored, no offense will be inflicted on the honor or the sovereignty of a great country such as England. There will be no seeking to lessen the legitimate prestige and the worthy patrimony of piety and usage proper to the Anglican Church when the Roman Catholic Church—this humble "Servant of the servants of God"—is able to embrace her ever beloved sister in the one authentic Communion of the family of Christ: a communion of origin and of faith, a communion of priesthood and of rule, a communion of the saints in the freedom and love of the spirit of Jesus.

Perhaps we shall have to go on, waiting and watching in prayer, in order to deserve that blessed day. But already we are strengthened in this hope by the heavenly friendship of the forty martyrs of England and Wales who are canonized today. Amen.

Two Saintly Profiles

Little John

POPE PAUL VI on October 25, 1970, canonized the Forty English Martyrs. Saints and martyrs are the true educators of mankind. They love and work for their fellowmen, but put God first. It is hoped that these English heroes and heroines will stimulate people of good will, especially the young, to a vision of life as an immensely worthwhile enterprise.

We do not suggest that present day Protestants are in any way responsible for the cruel persecution of Catholics in the 16th and 17th centuries, just as Protestants do not hold that present day Catholics are responsible for the burning to death of Protestants during the reign of Mary Tudor. Those days of intolerance and cruelty are happily things of the past, and we all regret them.

One of the most remarkable of the English martyrs was the Jesuit Brother, Nicholas Owen. If you had been staying with Mrs. Wiseman at Broadoaks in Essex in the winter of 1593, and had wakened about midnight, you might have heard a steady tapping noise coming from near the roof of the house. If you had asked at breakfast what the strange noise was Mrs. Wiseman would have answered, "Oh, that must have been our carpenter, Little

John, he has been building a stone fireplace in the Italian style in the living room." She spoke the truth. He had been doing this; but he had also been doing something else. He had been making a hiding place between the chapel above and the living room below.

By day he worked at the fashionable mantelpiece, but at night went to the chapel above and carefully excavated a hole in the solid brickwork, six feet deep and two feet wide, and cleverly concealed it. A few days later, Father John Gerard, the Jesuit superior, came to say Mass at Broadoaks. The Mass had been declared unlawful and priests, when caught, were executed. One of the servants, a traitor, informed the magistrate that a priest was in the house. Very early in the morning the house was surrounded and the magistrate banged on the door shouting, "Open in the Queen's name."

Mrs. Wiseman delayed long enough for Father Gerard to be concealed in the hiding place, then opened the door. The soldiers, headed by the magistrate, locked Mrs. Wiseman and her two daughters and the servants in one of the rooms, then made a thorough search of the house. They even measured the rooms with long rods to see if the lower rooms corresponded with the upper. They sounded the floors and walls looking for hollow places.

They knew a priest was in the house but no one, not even the traitor, knew where. Meanwhile, Father Gerard could hear every word they said when they were in the chapel or living room. In his hiding place had been put a jar of quince jelly and biscuits. He needed it, because the search lasted four days.

Suddenly, the searchers found a hiding place, and in it was a bottle of wine and store of food. This convinced them that the priest had left, and they ended the search. Little John had fooled them by constructing a dummy hiding place. Father Gerard emerged safely.

John then went to another famous house in Cambridge called Sawston Hall. It has tall towers, vast galleries, wide windows, great courtyards, and a dry moat. It also has several hiding holes, and these too were built by Little John and saved the lives of many priests.

Little John's real name was Nicholas Owen. He was very short in stature and his superior, Father John Gerard, very tall, so they called the one Little John and the other Long John. Nicholas was a highly skilled carpenter and builder and devoted himself entirely to the Jesuit missionary priests, especially Edmund Campion, John Gerard, and Henry Garnet. He himself was a Jesuit, not a priest but a Brother, that is, a member of the Order dedicated to helping the priests carry out their duties.

Today we are discovering hiding holes in the stately 16th century houses up and down England – the work of Nicholas Owen. He worked steadily for 26 years. He would accompany a priest to a mansion. There during the day he would do repairs but at night, when everyone was asleep, he would begin excavating the hiding hole. No one knew its position except the owner of the hiding hole. Sometimes he constructed a hiding hole within a hiding hole, so that if the priest-hunters discovered the outer one they might give up the search.

But three years later, Nicholas and Father Gerard were arrested. They were staying in London and were betrayed by a servant. Police burst into their bedroom and caught them. Nicholas was tortured for three hours and was ordered to give information about priests. He was silent. A Catholic gentleman, hearing of the arrest, offered money for their release. As Nicholas seemed unimportant he was allowed to go.

Father Gerard, however, was imprisoned in the Tower of London. Nicholas, now free, determined to rescue Father Gerard, and organized one of the most brilliant escapes that have been made from the famous Tower. Father Gerard and another Catholic prisoner were lodged in the high Cradle Tower overlooking the Thames River. There was a wharf opposite the Cradle Tower but separated from it by the river. At midnight two friends of Nicholas rowed up the Thames and landed on the wharf carrying a long rope. Father Gerard flung down an iron ball attached to a cord that had been smuggled in to him. The men on the wharf caught it and fastened the rope to the cord and Father Gerard pulled it to the top of the tower and made it fast. Then he and the other prisoner slid down the rope and were helped into the boat. They rowed downstream to an agreed landing place where Nicholas was waiting for them with horses, and they got away safely.

Nicholas went on with his underground activities for 11 more years. One of his most remarkable successes was at Baddesley Clinton in Warwickshire. His hideout there was so cleverly constructed that it is in perfect working order today. He found a large tunnel at the base of the west wing, running into a moat. It was a sewer. Nicholas diverted the sewage by another channel into the moat, and blocked up the original tunnel where it led into the moat by fixing a heavy stone at the exit, the same width as the tunnel. Then he constructed a sloping shaft, leading from the sacristy into the tunnel, which was now cut off from the moat. The entrance to this shaft he concealed by a window seat which can be lifted and is still there. When you lift up the seat all you can see is the floor, which looks like any other part of the floor. Actually, it is a trap-door leading into the sloping shaft.

The house belonged to Eleanor Vaux, a widow, and her sister Anne, who allowed the head Jesuit, Father Henry Garnet, to use it as his headquarters. In October, 1591, Father Garnet invited several other priests for a conference lasting four days. On the fourth day at 5:00 a.m., one of them, Father Southwell, was just about to begin Mass when priest-hunters began banging on the door. The priests, seizing the chalice and hosts, slid down the shaft and caught the vestments, books, Rosaries, and other religious articles which the Sisters threw after them. Meanwhile the priest-hunters were bawling and yelling outside, but the servants held the door fast, shouting that the mistress of the house, a widow, was not yet up but was coming down to answer them as soon as she could.

When all the priests were safely hidden, the door was opened and the priest-hunters let in. They rushed madly through the whole house, taking four hours over the work, but they found nothing and they departed. After a long interval (to make sure they were not coming back as they sometimes did) Eleanor Vaux called the priests out of the tunnel. "The hiding place was below ground level, the floor was covered with water and I was standing with my feet in it all the time," writes Father Garnet. All of them, five Jesuits, two secular priests, and three laymen owed their escape to the ingenuity of Nicholas Owen.

Then disaster happened. Some hotheaded young Catholics, exasperated by James I breaking his promise to grant toleration to Catholics, devised a wicked scheme to get rid of the King and Government by blowing up both houses of Parliament. The King's secretary, Robert Cecil, got to know about this harebrained plot and secretly encouraged it. It was just what he wanted in order to make everyone hate the Catholics, especially the Jesuits. At the right moment Cecil struck. He arrested Guy Fawkes and rounded up the other conspirators. He was anxious to capture the head Jesuit, Father Garnet, and incriminate him too. Father Garnet and Nicholas Owen discreetly retired to Hindlip Hall, near Worcester, a large house well provided with hiding holes. But Cecil traced Father Garnet to Hindlip Hall and gave urgent orders that the priest had to be arrested.

Very early in the morning 100 armed men surrounded the house and forced an entrance. Meanwhile Father Garnet and another priest were hustled into one hiding hole and Nicholas Owen and a friend into another. Unfortunately they had no time to take food with them. For a whole week the men searched, tapping every wall, and calling in expert carpenters and masons to help them. Several hideouts were found, empty. But the search went on. They were certain that Garnet was somewhere in the house and were determined to get him.

But Nicholas Owen and his friend were starving, so they decided on a desperate measure. They would slip out, and if caught, pretend to be the two priests, hoping that the priest-hunters would then be satisfied and go away. Their hideout was at one end of a long gallery. When the searchers were at the other end Nicholas and his companion noiselessly emerged, closed the entrance behind them, and crept away. But they were seen and captured. They tried to pass themselves off as servants of the house but in vain. "Who are you?" they were asked. "We are Catholics." "Are you priests?" "That is for you to prove." "Where have you been all this time?" "We have been hiding." "Where?" "We cannot say." The searchers did not believe that either of them was Father Garnet and continued the hunt for three more days. They almost tore down the interior of the house and finally discovered Father Garnet's hiding place.

Father Garnet and Owen were lodged in different cells in the Tower of London. By this time the authorities knew that Owen was intimately connected with the Jesuits and the hiding holes. Day after day he was taken down to the torture chamber in the vault beneath the White Tower. They put iron gauntlets on Owen's wrists and ordered him to climb two or three wicker steps. They then lifted his arms and put an iron bar through rings on his gauntlets and fastened it to the wall. They moved the steps and left him hanging by his wrists. They asked: "What hiding places have you made? What priests do you know? Where has Father Garnet stayed?" But Owen would say nothing.

On March 1, 1606, he was racked for the last time. For many years he had suffered from a rupture. To increase his pain and make him reveal his secrets they fastened weights to his feet. The strain on his stomach was so great that it burst open and his intestines came out. He was in great agony and died the following morning.

But he died with all his secrets locked in his brain, and years after his death priests and others were able to continue their work by means of his hiding holes. And even today, as the stately homes in England are being renovated, hiding places are often discovered.—*John Gallagher*, S.J.

Saint Margaret Clitherow

IF YOU HAD been in England on July 1, 1571, you would have heard great rejoicing at the home of the Sheriff of York, for it was the wedding-feast of his step-daughter, Margaret Middleton. What an attractive bride she was—18 years old, with her clear skin, long golden hair, charming personality!

Her husband, John Clitherow, was one of the most popular and prosperous men in the city. They went to live at The Shambles, with its red-tiled roof and huge oak beams. Margaret was busy running a large house, with its many maids and apprentices, brewing ale, curing Yorkshire hams, preserving jams, bringing up two step-children aged three and one. And by the time she was 21 she had two children of her own, Henry and Anne.

But they were sad days for the Catholics. Priests were killed, and Catholics attending Mass were heavily fined and imprisoned. Still the priests were there, saying Mass during the night, traveling around the country in disguise, hiding in Catholic homes.

Margaret, who was not a Catholic, had Catholic friends, and one day happened to meet a priest who was staying at one of the homes. She became so interested in Catholic teaching that she begged to hear it all and finally was received into the Church and became an enthusiastic Catholic.

Margaret taught the faith to her own children and others, and secretly arranged for priests to stay at The Shambles to say Mass and give the sacraments. Local Catholics were told of this and often would come to Margaret's house at night for midnight Mass. She even had a hiding-place built for the priest to slip into in case of danger.

All this, of course, was highly illegal, but Margaret was so universally loved and her Catholic activities were so carefully managed, that no one thought of danger. Her husband, John, was nominally a Catholic, but was ambitious, aspiring to be Lord Mayor, so found it more prudent to be seen attending the new Protestant services. However, he dearly loved his wife and didn't hinder her Catholic work in any way.

So Margaret was completely busy, and thoroughly enjoyed herself. Always full of fun and laughter her motto was that of St. Thomas More: "A man can live for the next world and yet be merry." She hadn't the slightest idea of the terrible tragedy that was about to befall her.

At the beginning of Queen Elizabeth's reign, the Government was becoming increasingly uneasy about the presence of Catholic priests in the country, and especially about the hated Jesuits. The Catholic religion, they said, should have been dead by this time, but instead of that, it was very much alive. They knew, too, that it was strong in the north, especially in York, and spies had informed them that the Clitherow family were the organizers.

They suddenly acted. John Clitherow was ordered to appear before the authorities for questioning, and at the same time a large group of police with a search warrant knocked on the door of The Shambles. John, who had often been seen at the new Protestant services, was let off lightly, but with Margaret, it was a very different story.

She and the servants were locked in one room and the children in another while the priest-hunters thoroughly ransacked the house. They could find no priest nor the slightest trace of one. Infuriated, they interrogated Margaret for hours, but got nothing from her.

Then they turned on the children. In spite of the bullying, they too stood firm. But one little Flemish boy, terrified when they threatened to flog him, broke down. He confessed that he had often seen priests in the house who had said Mass, and he showed them the hiding-place, fortunately empty, and Mass vestments and chalice used by the priest.

It was enough. The new law of Queen Elizabeth I said that anyone found helping a priest would, unless he renounced the Catholic faith, be put to death. Margaret was arrested; charged with "Harboring Jesuits and seminary priests, traitors to the Queen's Majesty."

At the trial Margaret denied that the priests were enemies of the Queen; "I have never harbored any but the Queen's friends, God forbid that I should." She refused to be tried by jury, though the judge warned her this would increase her suffering. "God's will be done," answered Margaret bravely, "I think I may suffer any death for this just cause."

She refused a jury because she knew this would consist of her own neighbors and friends, and the witnesses called would be her own children. She did not want to involve any of them in responsibility for her death. She said, "I know well that the jury must have found me guilty to please the Government which earnestly seeks my blood. Then they would all have been accessory to my death and grievously offended God. I thought it therefore charity on my part to hinder the jury from such a sin. And since it must needs be done, to cause as few to do it as might be, and that was the judge himself."

The judge passed sentence. "Margaret Clitherow, you must return from whence you came, and there in the lowest part of the prison be stripped naked, laid down, your back upon the ground, your hands and feet tied to posts, a sharp stone under your back and weights laid upon you and be pressed to death."

Margaret accepted this terrible fate calmly. "God be thanked. All that he shall send me shall be welcome. I have deserved death for mine offences to God, but not for anything I am accused of." The police then tied her arms with cords, and she was taken under guard to York prison.

She was not allowed to see either her husband or children but she managed to send her bonnet to her husband as a sign of her wifely duty to him, and to Anne her daughter she sent her shoes with the message, "Walk in these." Ministers of the new religion and other officials were the only people allowed to visit her.

On Friday, March 25, 1586, the sheriffs came for her at eight o'clock in the morning. Barefoot she stepped out of the prison to walk to the place of execution. The streets were packed, and the people were amazed to see Margaret looking so happy. The four officials who usually carried out executions refused to touch this case, so four beggars were hired.

Margaret knelt and prayed silently. She was ordered to pray for the Queen. She answered, "I pray especially for Queen Elizabeth that God may turn her to the Catholic faith and that after this mortal life she may receive the blessed joys of heaven." When told to confess that she died for treason she answered, "No, I die for the love of my lord Jesus."

Very quietly she lay down upon the floor. A sharp stone the size of a man's fist was placed under her back. A door was put on her and on this the four beggars laid heavy weights. She whispered, "Jesus, have mercy upon me," and repeated this again and again. Her agony lasted 15 minutes, then the moaning stopped, and all was quiet.

This cruel execution shocked the people of York, who had known and loved Margaret. Far from discouraging them in their Catholic faith it had the opposite effect. They were inspired by her death. Her children were worthy of her. Anne refused to join the new religion, escaped to the Continent and became a nun working for missionary priests. Both boys, William and Henry, became priests and continued Margaret's work.—*John Gallagher, S.J.*

The 40 New Martyr Saints

St. John Houghton, priest, Carthusian monk, prior of London Charterhouse; died, Tyburn, May 4, 1535.

St. Robert Lawrence, priest, Carthusian monk, prior of Beauvale, Notts; died, Tyburn, May 4, 1535.

St. Augustine Webster, priest, Carthusian monk, prior of Axholme, Lincs; died, Tyburn, May 4, 1535.

St. Richard Reynolds, priest, Bridgettine monk of Syon Abbey, Mddx.; died, Tyburn, May 4, 1535.

St. John Stone, priest, Augustinian monk of Austin Friars, Canterbury; died Canterbury, not later than Dec. 29, 1539.

St. Cuthbert Mayne, sem. priest. Condemned under Act of Supremacy and for priesthood; died Launceston, Nov. 30, 1577.

St. Edmund Campion, priest. Condemned for the fictitious plot in Rome and Flanders; died, Tyburn, Dec. 1, 1581.

St. Ralph Sherwin, sem. priest. Condemned for the fictitious plot in Rome and Flanders; died, Tyburn, Dec. 1, 1581.

St. Alexander Briant, sem. priest. Condemned for the fictitious plot in Rome and Flanders; died, Tyburn, Dec. 1, 1581

St. John Paine, sem. priest. Condemned for the fictitious plot in Rome and Flanders; died, Chelmsford, April 2, 1582.

St. Luke Kirby, sem. priest. Condemned for the fictitious plot in Rome and Flanders; died, Tyburn, May 30, 1582.

St. Richard Gwyn, layman; schoolmaster in Flints and Denbighshire; died, Wrexham, Oct. 17, 1584.

St. Margaret Clitherow, laywoman; convert and receiver of priests. Pressed to death; died, York, March 25, 1586.

St. Margaret Ward, laywoman. Condemned for rescuing a priest. Hanged; died, Tyburn, Aug. 30, 1588.

St. Edmund Gennings, sem. priest. Condemned for priesthood; Gray's Inn Fields, Dec. 10, 1591.

St. Swithun Wells, layman. Hanged for harboring Gennings; died, Gray's Inn Fields, Dec. 10, 1591.

St. Eustace White, sem. priest. Condemned for priesthood; died, Tyburn, Dec. 10, 1591.

St. Polydore Plasden, sem. priest. Condemned for priesthood; died, Tyburn, Dec. 10, 1591.

St. John Boste, sem. priest. Condemned for priesthood; died,

Durham, July 24, 1594.

St. Robert Southwell, priest. Condemned for priesthood; died, Tyburn, Feb. 21, 1595.

St. Henry Walpole, priest. Condemned for priesthood; died, Warwick, August 13, 1595.

St. Philip Howard, Earl of Arundel, layman; prisoner until sentence of death for being reconciled, 1585 until death; died, Tower of London, Oct. 19, 1595.

St. John Jones, priest, Franciscan. Condemned for priesthood; died, Southwark, July 12, 1598.

St. John Rigby, layman. Condemned for being reconciled; died, Southwark, June 21, 1600.

St. Anne Line, laywoman. Hanged for harboring; died, Tyburn, Feb. 27, 1601.

St. Nicholas Owen, Jesuit brother, companion to Father Henry Garnet, S.J., died from torture; died, Tower of London, March 2, 1606.

St. Thomas Garnet, priest. Condemned for priesthood; died, Tyburn, June 23, 1608.

St. John Roberts, priest. Condemned for priesthood; died, Tyburn, Dec. 10, 1610.

St. John Almond, sem. priest. Condemned for priesthood; died, Tyburn, Dec. 5, 1612.

St. Edmund Arrowsmith, priest. Condemned for priesthood and "persuading to popery"; died, Lancaster, Aug. 28, 1628.

St. Ambrose (Edward) Barlow, priest. Condemned for priesthood; died, Lancaster, Sept. 10, 1641.

St. Alban (Bartholomew) Roe (Rowe), priest. Condemned for priesthood; died, Tyburn, Jan. 31, 1642.

St. Henry Morse, priest. Condemned for priesthood; died, Tyburn, Feb. 1, 1645.

St. John Southworth, sem. priest. Condemned for priesthood; died, Tyburn, June 28, 1654.

St. John (or William) Plessington (Pleasington), sem. priest. Condemned for priesthood; died, Chester, July 19, 1679.

St. Philip Evans, priest. Condemned for priesthood; died, Cardiff, July 22, 1679.

St. John Lloyd, sem. priest. Condemned for priesthood; died, Cardiff, July 22, 1679.

St. John Wall, priest. Condemned for priesthood; died, Worchester, Aug. 22, 1679.

St. John Kemble, sem. priest. Condemned for priesthood; died, Hereford, Aug. 22, 1679.

St. David Lewis, priest. Condemned for priesthood; died, Usk, Aug. 27, 1679.

OTHER BOOKS FROM OUR SUNDAY VISITOR

THE FUTURE PARISH

By Rev. Richard Currier, *paper* 95¢

Father Currier does not believe that the need for Christian community can be met in large parishes of 500 families or more. He sees the solution in what he calls neighborhood parishes, arising from current research in scripture and investigations in theology. The book is not based on wishful thinking or unrealized dreams. It has resulted from long and careful experimentation in the Diocese of Lansing and Saginaw.

HAPPINESS OVER THE HILL

By Rev. Joseph E. Manton, C.SS.R., *cloth* $4.95, *paper* $1.95

Reflections for everyday Christian living. Stories of saints and sinners and situations. Thoughts about our Lord and our Lady.

WHAT CATHOLICS BELIEVE TODAY

By Msgr. Paul Poupard, *paper* 95¢

Addressed to all those who are baptized and intended to help them know the Catholic Faith better. Soul-searching writings on The Mystery of God, The Joy of Believing, On the Way to Eternity, Hope, and more. Includes Pope Paul VI's Prayer for Faith.

THE CATHOLIC RELIGION

By Most Rev. Bernard D. Stewart, Bishop of Sandhurst, Australia, *paper* $1.25

An outline of Catholic doctrine from statements made by Pope Paul VI and by Vatican Council II concerning fundamental truths of the Catholic Religion. The table of contents are very complete. Included are the corrections to be made to the New Dutch Catechism and answers suggested to some current questions raised in lectures on religious doctrine.

If your bookseller does not have these titles, you may order them by sending listed price (we pay postage and handling) to the Book Department at the address below. Enclose check or money order — do not send cash.

Write for free book list

Our Sunday Visitor, Inc. / Noll Plaza / Huntington, Ind. 46750